ROCK BANDS

JH RICE

Badger Publishing Limited
Oldmedow Road,
Hardwick Industrial Estate,
King's Lynn PE30 4JJ
Telephone: 01438 791037

www.badgerlearning.co.uk

2 4 6 8 10 9 7 5 3 1

Rock Bands ISBN 978-1-78464-000-2

Text © JH Rice 2014

Complete work © Badger Publishing Limited 2014

Publisher: Susan Ross
Senior Editor: Danny Pearson
Publishing Assistant: Claire Morgan
Designer: Fiona Grant
Series Consultant: Dee Reid

Photos: Cover Image:Vanja Ivosevic
Page 5: GEORGE KONIG/REX
Page 6: Everett Collection/REX
Page 7: Everett Collection/REX
Page 8: Alan Messer/REX
Page 10: © CBW/Alamy
Page 11: Barry Schultz/Sunshine/REX
Page 13: © AF archive/Alamy
Page 14: © Reimar 4/Alamy
Page 15: Broadimage/REX
Page 16: View Pictures/REX
Page 17: Patrick O'Leary/REX
Page 18: © WENN Ltd/Alamy
Page 19: © ZUMA Press, Inc./Alamy
Page 20: David Magnus/REX
Page 27: MARC SHARRATT/REX
Page 28: REX
Page 30: Joby Sessions/Future Publish/REX

Contents

1.	The first rock bands	5
3.	Glam rock, punk and metal	8
3.	Rock	16
4.	Instruments	20
	Questions	31
	Index	32

Vocabulary

amplified   instruments
complicated   lightning
dyed   rhythm
independent   stadium

1. THE FIRST ROCK BANDS

Rock bands started playing in the 1950s.

One of the first bands was Bill Haley and His Comets.

They played a style of music that was based on a mix of rhythm and blues, swing and country music.

The music was fast and loud. It made people want to dance and teenagers loved the music.

The biggest rock star of the 1950s and 1960s was Elvis Presley.

He had 18 Number 1 hits. Elvis used to twist his hips when he sang and he was nicknamed 'Elvis the Pelvis'!

WOW! facts

Elvis Presley has sold more than one billion albums.

Elvis was so popular he became known as 'The King'.

On stage he wore jumpsuits. He dyed his hair black and wore lots of hair gel.

Elvis starred in 31 films. Some people thought the films were not very good but fans of The King thought they were great!

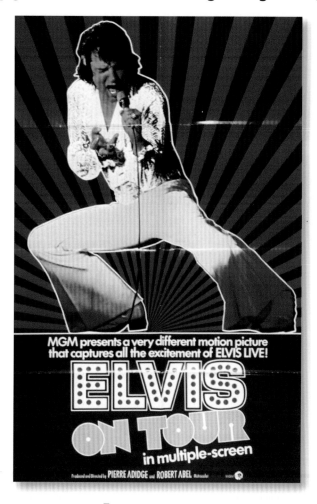

2. GLAM ROCK, PUNK AND METAL

Over time, different bands began to make their own style of rock music. Some changed the way they played. Some started wearing really wacky outfits!

Glam rock

Glam rock bands liked to shock their fans...

They wore:
- wild clothes
- crazy hairstyles
- lots of make-up

Famous glam rock bands:
- T. Rex
- Wizzard
- Alice Cooper

David Bowie was a very popular rock star in the 1970s.

He sang as two different people: Ziggy Stardust and
Aladdin Sane. Both Ziggy Stardust and Aladdin Sane
had dyed red hair.

Bowie wore make-up like a lightning flash across his
face. The heels on his platform boots were over
17 centimetres high.

Bowie has sold over 140 million albums!

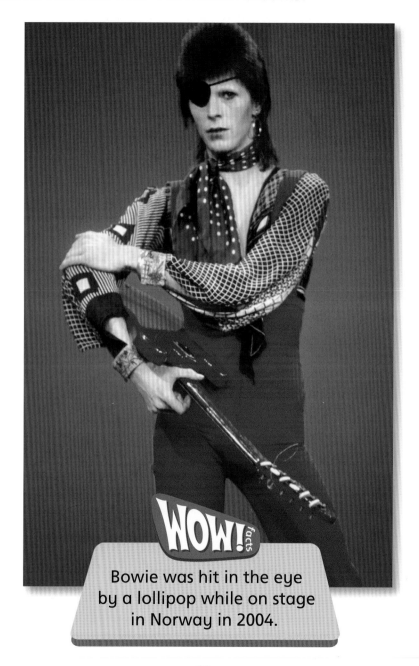

WOW! facts

Bowie was hit in the eye
by a lollipop while on stage
in Norway in 2004.

Punk rock

Punk rock came after glam rock and was even more wild!

Punk rockers wore:
- torn clothes
- safety pins (in their clothes and bodies)
- Dr. Martens boots
- spiky hair

Punk rock had short, fast, angry songs.

Sometimes, the people in a band could not even play their instruments!

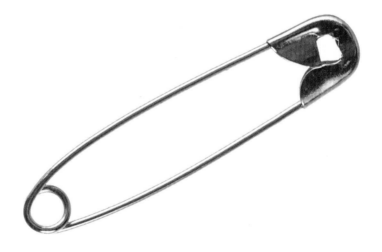

Famous punk rock bands:

- The Clash
- Dead Kennedys
- Sex Pistols
- The Ramones

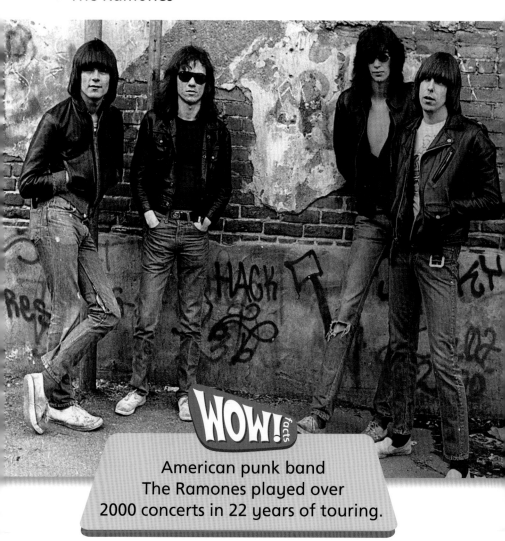

WOW! facts

American punk band
The Ramones played over
2000 concerts in 22 years of touring.

Heavy metal

Heavy metal bands are loud!

The music has:
- strong drum beats
- long guitar solos
- singers who can really hit the high notes

Heavy metal fans often wear studded black leather jackets or vests. They may also wear heavy rings and chains.

Ozzy Osbourne, lead singer of Black Sabbath, is known to millions because a very popular reality show was made about his family.

Other famous heavy metal bands:
- Metallica
- Motorhead
- Iron Maiden
- AC/DC

WOW! facts

Ozzy Osbourne has homemade tattoos of smiley faces on his knees!

3. ROCK

Stadium rock

Some rock bands are so popular that only a stadium is big enough to hold all the people who want to see them play.

Stadium (or arena) tours are huge events. Some stadiums can hold 90,000 fans.

Between 2009 and 2011, U2 held the U2 360° Tour.

An enormous set called The Claw was built in the middle of each stadium that the band visited.

U2 360° Tour facts and figures

- 120 trucks were used to transport the set.
- The Claw was 51 metres tall.
- Each structure cost over £15 million to build.
- There were 110 concerts.
- 30 countries were visited.
- 7.2 million tickets were sold.

Indie rock

'Indie' is short for independent. Indie rock is used to describe bands that have recorded and sold their music without the help of one of the big music groups.

Kaiser Chiefs were signed to an independent record label in 2003.

Daft Punk are a French duo. They were first signed by an independent company.

The virtual band Gorillaz was created by Damon Albarn (lead singer and keyboardist of Blur) and cartoonist Jamie Hewlett.

The virtual members of the band were:
Murdoc Niccals – bass guitar and drum machine

Noodle – guitar, keyboard and backing vocals

2D – lead vocalist, keyboard and melodica

Russel Hobbs – drums and percussion

If you had the chance to create a rock group, what would it look like? Who would you want to be in it?

4. INSTRUMENTS

Lots of different instruments have been used in rock bands, from bagpipes (AC/DC) to violins (Linkin Park), but all rock bands use guitars, drums and vocals.

The Beatles

Ringo Starr – drums

Paul McCartney – bass guitar and vocals

George Harrison – lead guitar and vocals

John Lennon – rhythm guitar and vocals

Guitars

There are lots of different types of guitar.

In the early days, rock bands used semi-acoustic guitars with steel strings, which were plucked with a pick.

The sound was amplified by plugging the guitar into an electrical amplifier and a speaker.

Some semi-acoustic guitars have 12 strings.

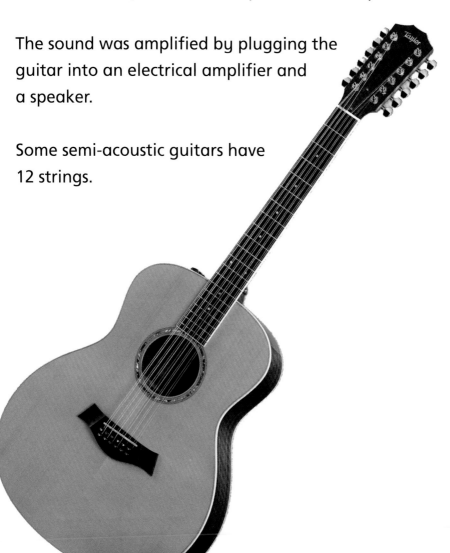

Electric guitars are played like semi-acoustic guitars.

The steel strings are plucked with a pick.

Most electric guitars have six strings.

They can make the really loud sound that rock bands like.

As they are not hollow, they can be made into different shapes.

Lead guitarists play the melody or tune of a song.

They also play guitar solos – this is when they can show off their skills.

Great lead guitarists

Guitarist	Band
Eric Clapton	**Cream**
Jimi Hendrix	**The Jimi Hendrix Experience**
Brian May	**Queen**
Jimmy Page	**Led Zeppelin**
Keith Richards	**The Rolling Stones**
Slash	**Guns N' Roses**

Slash's real name is Saul Hudson – not such a good name for a wild rock band leader!

Rhythm guitar

The rhythm guitar has six strings like the lead guitar, but it is not played the same way.

The rhythm guitarist plays chords and riffs while the lead guitarist is playing the tune.

Rhythm guitars are amplified like the lead guitar.

Bass guitar

The bass guitar has four strings.

These strings are thicker than the strings on a normal guitar.

The notes on the bass guitar are much deeper than the lead guitar.

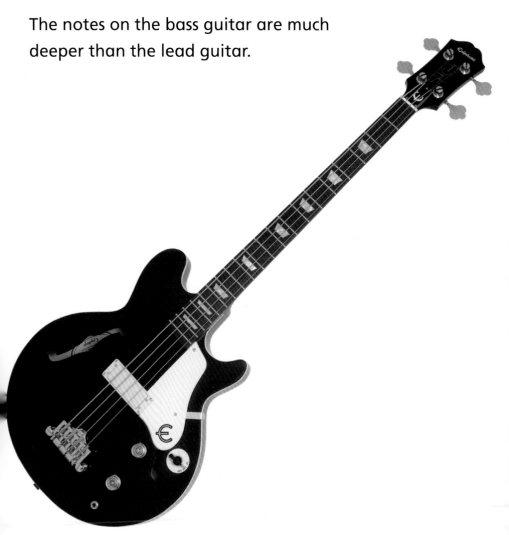

Bass guitars keep the beat in rock music. They play the bass note of chords and can also be heard playing complicated riffs and licks.

Bass guitars can be played in different ways: by slapping, tapping or popping the strings.

Great bass players

Name	Band
John Entwistle	**The Who**
Flea	**Red Hot Chili Peppers**
Phil Lynott	**Thin Lizzy**

The most expensive bass guitar cost over £150,000!

Lots of guitar players, like Jimi Hendrix and Paul McCartney, are left-handed.

To make it easier to play, they string the guitar the other way round and use their left hand to strum and their right hand to form the chords.

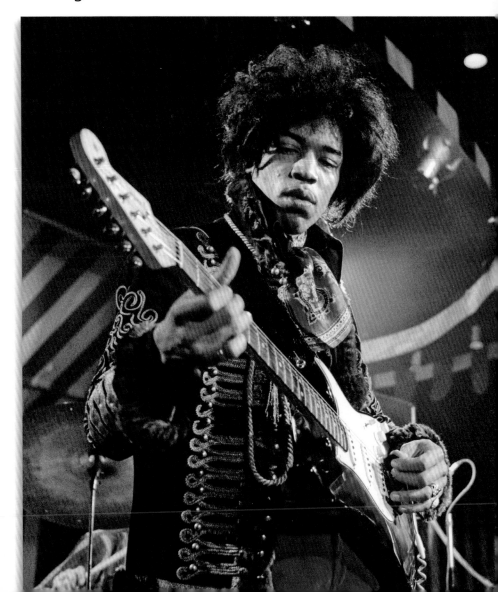

Drums

Drums are very important in a rock band. They provide the rhythm and drive.

Without drums it just wouldn't be a rock band!

Drummers don't just play the drums with their hands. They use their feet too!

The bass drum and hi-hat are both worked by foot pedals.

Drummers must have great rhythm.

They practise making different sound patterns with their hands and their feet.

It's easy to hit a drum, but not so easy to set and keep a rhythm for your band.

Great drummers

Drummer	Band
John Bonham	**Led Zeppelin**
Keith Moon	**The Who**
Phil Collins	**Genesis**
Dave Grohl	**Nirvana/Foo Fighters**

How many drums can a drummer play?

Neil Peart from the band Rush plays a drum kit
containing 42 drums!

Rick Allen of Def Leppard lost his arm
in a car crash, but that did not stop him from
drumming. His nickname is 'The Thunder God'.

Questions

Name the biggest rock star of the 1950s and 1960s. *(page 6)*

What year was David Bowie hit in the eye with a lollipop? *(page 11)*

Can you name three heavy metal bands? *(page 15)*

What instrument did Ringo Starr play? *(page 20)*

What band was Slash a part of? *(page 23)*

How many drums are in Neil Peart's drum kit? *(page 30)*

INDEX

AC/DC 15, 20
Allen, Rick 30
bass guitar 19, 25-26
Beatles, The 20
Bill Haley and His Comets 5
Bowie, David 10-11
Daft Punk 18
drum(s) 19, 20, 28, 30
electric guitar 22
glam rock 8, 12
Gorillaz 19
guitar 14, 19, 20, 21-27
heavy metal 14-15
Hendrix, Jimi 23, 27
indie rock 18
Kaiser Chiefs 18
lead guitarists 23, 24
Led Zeppelin 23, 29
McCartney, Paul 20, 27
Osbourne, Ozzy 15
Peart, Neil 30
Presley, Elvis 6-7
punk rock 12-13
Ramones, The 13
rhythm guitar 20, 24
semi-acoustic guitar 21, 22
stadium 16, 17
U2 360° Tour 17
Who, The 26, 29